GOLDEN PEANUT

FILIPINO HUMOR
FOR MANY OCCASIONS

JUANITO M. JAMORA

FriesenPress

Suite 300 - 990 Fort St
Victoria, BC, V8V 3K2
Canada

www.friesenpress.com

ISBN
978-1-5255-6796-4 (Hardcover)
978-1-5255-6797-1 (Paperback)
978-1-5255-6798-8 (eBook)

1. HUMOR, TOPIC, RELIGION

Distributed to the trade by The Ingram Book Company

This book is dedicated to the ever living and loving God, my Creator: the source of all that I am, all that I have, and all that I can do. To Him be all the honor and glory!

1. CHILDREN'S CATECHISM CLASS

During a catechism class, the priest told his students, "Children, in hell there will be weeping and gnashing of teeth."

A boy asked, "Father, Father, how about those who died without teeth?"

The priest answered, "Those, my son, will be provided."

2. SAYING THE ROSARY WHILE SMOKING A CIGARETTE

At break time from their Spiritual Retreat, a young boy asked their retreat master, "Father, is it all right to smoke cigarettes while saying the rosary?"

The priest answered, "Oh no, my son, do not desecrate your prayer time by smoking a cigarette."

Another boy approached the same priest asking him, "Father, is it all right to say the rosary while smoking a cigarette?"

He answered, "Oh yes, my son, you should pray always, even during your recreation time."

3. WHO ELSE?

In one of their romantic moments, Eve asked, "Adam, am I still the woman you are really in love with?

Adam just shrugged saying, "Who else?"

4. WHY DID GOD CREATE EVE BEAUTIFUL?

One day Adam asked God, "Lord, why did you create Eve beautiful?"

"So that you can love her," God answered.

Adam continued, "And, why did you create her stupid?"

He replied, "So that she can love you."

5. THE PROPHET JONAH

Given the rebellious nature of Prophet Jonah, Pedro and Jose could not agree on whether he went to heaven or to hell. Finally, Pedro concluded, "I am sure Jonah went to heaven. When I die, I will ask him."

"What if he went to hell?" Jose protested.

Pedro said, "Then when you die, you will ask him."

6. PRACTICAL ADVICE TO A PARISH PRIEST

A parishioner who went to the rectory was surprised to see the parish priest with a bleeding chin. "What happened to you, Father?" he asked.

The priest answered, "I accidentally cut my chin when I was shaving, while I was thinking about my long sermon for this coming Sunday mass."

The parishioner said, "My advice to you, Father, is cut down your sermon and concentrate on your shaving."

7. TERRIBLE STAGE FRIGHT

A brand-new priest has terrible stage fright. Every time he delivers his sermon he falls down unconscious.

The bishop took pity on the young priest and advised him, "My son, to cure your stage fright, try to arrest the attention of the congregation by stating something outrageous, like saying, 'I've fallen in love with a woman.' Then, later on, you declare her name is Mary, our Blessed Mother Virgin Mary."

The next time the young priest went to deliver his sermon, before he knew it, he succumbed to his usual terrible stage fright. As he was falling down, before losing his consciousness, he was able to shout at the top of his voice, "The bishop is in love with a woman and her name is Mary!" Then he fell down to the floor fully unconscious.

8. A CATHOLIC DOG

One day a wealthy elderly lady approached a parish priest, asking him if her dog could be buried in the Catholic cemetery.

He answered, "Oh no, Lady, it is unheard of that a dog would be buried in a Catholic cemetery. Why don't you try asking the Protestant minister across the street?"

The lady, opening her check book as she was leaving, asked the priest, "Father, do you think $10,000 would be an acceptable amount to pay for my dog's burial in the Protestant cemetery?"

Before she went through the rectory gate, the priest called her back. "Lady, please wait! You didn't tell me that your beloved pet was a Catholic dog."

9. LANDING IN HEAVEN

One day, a charismatic reborn person died. Because of his devout life while living here on earth, he could only hover just above heaven, but could never quite land. So, St. Peter, looking up, shouted to him, "For heaven's sake, say a bad word!"

10. THE SECRET TO ENTERING HEAVEN

Right after her death, the woman appeared before St. Peter who told her, "You people on earth think that it is difficult to enter heaven. Nothing is farther from the truth. To enter heaven, all you have to do is spell the word 'love'." Having spelled it correctly, the woman got admitted into heaven.

One day after several years, St. Peter told her, "I was called by Jesus for a conference. Please man the door to heaven until my return. You already know the ground rules for admission into heaven."

After St. Peter left, she noticed a very familiar figure approaching at a distance. Indeed, she saw it was her husband! He was very excited and happy to see his wife, who without delay told him the secret to getting into heaven: "It is easy to enter heaven. All you have to do is spell a word."

Very eagerly, the husband asked, "What word do you want me to spell, dear?"

She replied, "Spell, 'Czechoslovakia'."

11. PRAYING INSTEAD OF SLEEPING

A priest and a taxi driver, who died at the same time, appeared together before St. Peter whose judgement was to send the former to purgatory and the latter to heaven.

The priest complained, "St. Peter, it would be unfair that you send me, a man of God, to purgatory, while you allow that worldly taxi driver to go to heaven. While on earth, I brought people closer to God, whereas that taxi driver most likely transported shady characters such as murderers, prostitutes, drug lords, and so forth.

St. Peter answered, "The thing is, while you were on earth, your sermons were so boring that the majority of your congregation fell asleep as you were talking. The taxi driver, however, was so reckless that his passengers were praying instead of sleeping."

12. JUMPING TO CONCLUSIONS

During a meeting with his parishioners a parish priest was asked by a young man, "Father, what is the cause of arthritis?"

Having known the man to have been indulging in vices such as womanizing, drinking, gambling and behaving irresponsibly towards his family, the parish priest, thinking that that this is a rare opportunity to evangelize him, answered, "When a man is a womanizer, drinker, gambler, and being irresponsible, sooner or later he will develop arthritis. And why are you asking me this question, my son? "

He answered, "Because, Father, yesterday I read in the newspaper that Pope Francis has arthritis."

13. CARRY YOUR CROSS

Upon getting home from attending a charismatic seminar the husband immediately picked his wife up. She said, "I can tell, dear, that the topic of your seminar must have been 'Love.'"

He said, "No, our seminar's topic was 'Carry your cross.'"

14. THE CORNER LOT

Right after his death, the businessman appeared before St. Peter, who mapped his eternal destination alternatives for him.

"Mr. Businessman," he said, "you choose where to go. We are here at the crossroads. If you go straight you will definitely end up in purgatory. If you turn right, you will certainly reach heaven, but if you turn left you will surely go to hell. Where do you want to go?"

He answered right away, "I'll just stay here right where I am."

"You want to just stay here? Why won't you proceed?" asked St. Peter.

The businessman insisted, "Because a corner lot is the best location for business."

15. THROWING PEANUT INTO THE WATER

Six young boys confessed to a priest, one after the other. The boys' almost identical confession was, "Father, I'm truly sorry that I threw peanut into the water. Please forgive me my sin."

The priest told each one of them, "Throwing peanut into the water is not a sin. Next time you throw peanut into the water, you don't have to confess it."

The seventh boy, gasping for breath, arrived to the confessional box. Before he could say anything, the priest barked at him, "Did you also throw peanut into the water?"

The boy answered, "No, Father, I am Peanut!"

16. MY WIFE SAID SO

One day, in heaven, men were asked to fall into one of two lines: 1) Undomesticated Husbands and 2) Domesticated Husbands.

Numerous men stood in the second line. Among the few standing in the first line was a henpecked husband. When the angel asked him, "Are you sure you belong to this line?" his instant reply was, "Oh, yes, my wife said so!"

17. ST. PETER'S DENIAL OF JESUS

Some people in the Holy Land believed that St. Peter denied Jesus because Jesus healed St. Peter's mother in law.

18. A HUSBAND'S BIBLICAL QUOTATION

A husband, unhappy about his situation, shouted within his domineering wife's hearing distance, "What God has joined together, let no one put us under!"

19. WHO WANTS TO GO TO HEAVEN NOW?

During one evening prayer meeting held inside the church, the priest asked the prayer group members, "Who of you want to go to heaven?" All of them raised their hands.

Then the priest asked them again, "Who of you want to go to heaven now?" This time nobody raised his or her hand.

20. ACT OF CONTRITION

A pilot noticed his airplane's engine was malfunctioning. He decided to make an emergency landing, first exhausting its fuel to avoid combustion by circling the intended landing spot a few times.

The passengers were already panicky when the pilot, knowing that the engine had already run out of fuel, tersely announced, "Attention all crews and passengers, our plane is now descending for an emergency belly landing. Everybody, be calm and repeat after me: "Oh my God, I am heartily sorry for having offended you and I detest all my sins . . ."

21. IS THAT SO?

A woman accused a holy priest of being the father of the baby she carried in her womb. The bishop confronted him, "You are accused by a pregnant woman that you impregnated her." His only reply was, "Is that so?"

Months later, on her deathbed the woman, who was dying of cancer, confessed that she had maliciously and falsely accused the priest, and that the real truth was that another man was actually the father of her baby.

The bishop broke the news to the accused, "You were absolved by the woman who accused you." "Is that so?" was the priest's same reply.

22. LORD, SUMUKO KA NA (LORD, YOU SURRENDER NOW)

In the Philippines, Ben, was among those who participated in the Cursillo (De Colores) class. When the little course about Christianity was about to be concluded, the rector invited each participant to talk and surrender everything to the Lord. But Ben's version of surrender was different. In front of very large Lord's image he declared, "Lord, *sumuko ka na, napaligiran ka na namin!*" (Lord, you surrender now, you are surrounded by many of us.)

23. BLOWING MOOD

A beloved pope was diagnosed to have a rare, life-threatening, heart disease. To save his life he would need an immediate heart transplant. The head cardinal announced this tragic news from the pope's window to a gathering below of several thousands of faithful Catholic supporters of the Holy Father.

In order to save the pope, many of them volunteered to donate their living hearts for transplantation. The cardinal dropped a very light, white feather down. It was agreed that on whomever the feather landed, that person would be the designated live heart donor.

The dropped feather floated on the air, gradually descending and changing its position with the breeze. Each one of the faithful below, putting their right palm on their left chest, said somewhat like this: "Take out my heart that my beloved pope may live!" and then they blew the air above them to keep the dreaded white feather from falling on them.

24. LET THE PERSON WHO HAS NO SIN CAST THE FIRST STONE

A story is told in the Bible about an adulterous woman caught committing adultery. In front of many people, she was brought by the scribes and Pharisees to Jesus. They asked him, "Teacher, this woman was caught in the very act of committing adultery. Now in the law, Moses required us to stone such a woman. What must we do?"

Jesus replied, "Let the person who is without sin be the first to throw a stone at her." In response the people went away one by one, beginning with the elders.

This story was later added to: At this moment, Jesus heard a stone passing by his ear. He turned around and saw his mother, the Immaculate Virgin Mary.

25. RETURNING AFTER USE

A priest complained to his houseboy, "Lando, why is it that our toothpick supply is fast running low?"

Lando quickly answered, "I don't know, Father, because each time I use toothpick I return it."

26. VATICAN II CHANGES

The old priest was told by the younger one, "Father, important changes have come out of the Second Vatican Ecumenical Council."

The old priest quickly dismissed them saying, "I don't care about those changes. I am already old and as the saying goes, 'You cannot teach an old dog new tricks.' "

"But what if one of those changes is priests are now allowed to marry?" asked the young priest.

"In that case, I am all in for that!" the old priest declared.

27. THE POPE DRIVING A TAXI

The pope befriended the driver and made an unusual request, "I am bored. Please allow me to drive this taxi."

"Okay, Your Holiness, I'll just stay at in the back, like your passenger, while you drive," said the taxi driver.

Minutes later, the pope was stopped for a minor traffic violation. The companions of the traffic officer begged him not to issue the ticket, "Please don't issue the pope a ticket! His passenger might be God!"

28. AND ALSO WITH YOU

Before, practically whatever the priest said in the mass, the congregation's reply was, "And also with you."

One Sunday mass, the priest was having a hard time with the microphone and remarked, "There is something wrong with this mic."

The congregation replied, "And also with you." That is the reason, according to some people, this reply is now changed to "And with your spirit."

29. LET PEOPLE ENTER HEAVEN THROUGH THE WINDOWS

One day, Jesus made a surprise audit of St. Peter's record of those who entered heaven compared to the actual total population in heaven.

He asked, "Peter, why is it that there are more people in heaven than the total number of those who entered heaven according to your record?"

"I don't know, Lord. Ask your mother, the Blessed Virgin Mary, because I have observed several times that she allowed many people to enter heaven through the windows!" reported St. Peter.

30. A BOHOLANO IN HEAVEN

Pablo, a Boholano or native of Bohol, one of the islands in the Philippines well-known for its beauty, died and went straight to heaven. St. Peter approached and told him, "I want you to go back to earth. It is not yet time for you to die. You are here because I made a mistake and pushed the wrong button."

"There's no way that I will agree to go back to earth. It is a thousand-fold sweeter living here in heaven," Pablo asserted.

Jesus happened to be passing by, and perceiving St. Peter's dilemma, he called Pablo over and whispered something to him. Right away, Pablo packed up his personal belongings, very much excited to go back to earth.

After Pablo left, St. Peter asked Jesus, "Lord, what was your secret way to convince him to immediately and enthusiastically want to go back to earth? I tried hard to persuade him to return, but to no avail."

"I just asked him, 'Pablo, are you not going home for your town fiesta next week?'" Jesus confided.

(Most Boholanos would relish the idea, and look forward to going back home for their town or barrio fiesta).

31. WHAT IS IT?

A husband gives it to his wife. The pope has it, but does not use it. What is it?

Answer: A family name.

32. PAMATION TA ANG PARI (LET'S KILL THE PRIEST)

In the Philippines, the two biggest regional dialects are Tagalog, mostly spoken in Manila, and Bisaya, mostly spoken in Cebu. One day, a Tagalog lector relocated from Manila to Cebu.

On his first Sunday mass in Cebu, before the large congregation, he read this message from his notes: *"Mga katawhan sa Dios,"* (People of God) *"maningdog kitang tanan"* (let us all rise) *"ug pamation ta ang pari"* (and let us kill the priest). The whole congregation broke out in boisterous laughter.

He should have pronounced the word *"pamation"* as *"pamati-on,"* meaning "to listen to." His message should properly have been: "People of God, let us all rise and listen to the priest."

33. NO NEED TO CONFESS AGAIN

Rey confessed to the priest, "Father, I have stolen a bunch of bananas. I am truly sorry, forgive me of my sin."

"Your penance, my son, is say one *Our Father* and one *Hail Mary*," the priest said.

He asked, "Father, instead of just one, can I say, two *Our Fathers* and two *Hail Marys*?"

"Why?" asked the surprised priest.

Rey answered, "So that I can go back to steal another bunch of bananas with no need to confess again."

34. THE RISK OF DOING A GOOD DEED

Roy, a sacristan, saved the life of a dying crocodile by boldly removing a large piece of wood that had got stuck up in the crocodile's mouth. For saving his life, the crocodile offered to take

the young man on a tour around the lake on his back. Roy accepted the offer, but only to go across the lake, not around it.

When they got to the middle of the lake, the crocodile declared, "I am very tired and hungry, so I am going to eat you for my lunch."

Terrified, Roy tried to compose himself. "Is that how you will repay my good deed of saving your life—by devouring me?"

The crocodile insisted, "Yes, in our world a good deed is repaid with punishment. Since your values are opposite to ours, let us ask three witnesses. If the majority of the opinions favor the values of the amphibian world, you will be eaten by me, but if it is the other way around, you will go scot-free."

The first witness they saw was a floating worn out basket. The crocodile asked, "Basket, should good deeds be repaid with rewards or with punishment?"

The basket replied, "Of course, good deeds should be repaid with punishments. Look at what happened to me. When I was new, my owner always cleaned me and put me in a sanitary place. Now that I am old and worn out, I have been just thrown away!"

The second witness that came along was an old floating shoe, which when asked the same question by the crocodile, gave a similar sad testimony. It also concluded that good deeds deserve punishment.

The crocodile then proudly announced, "Whatever the third witness says, I now have the majority of the three opinions. Let us ask the third witness so that the decision will favor me unanimously."

By now, they had reached the other side of the lake, where a bird was perching on the branch of a huge tree extending over the sea. "Bird!" shouted the crocodile, "Should good deeds be rewarded or punished?"

The bird kept saying, "I can't hear your voice above the sound of the waves!" The bird was hopping along the branch towards land, and the crocodile, with Roy on his back, was following it.

While Roy's attention was fixed on listening to the conversation between the two, the bird whispered to him, "What are you doing? You are now on land! Run for your life!" Instantly, Roy jumped off the crocodile and ran for safety, leaving behind the hungry and frustrated crocodile.

35. JUNIOR, WHERE IS YOUR DAD?

Daniel, before gambling, went to church to pray to the statue of St. Anthony. "St. Anthony, please help me win at gambling."

In the cockpit, however, he lost so much money that he decided to go back to St. Anthony and complain. The priest, noticing him approaching the church and fuming mad, ran inside and swapped the big St. Anthony statue with one that was much smaller.

Before the statue, the gambler shouted, "Junior, where is your dad?"

36. A KILLER'S CONFESSION

A killer confessed to the priest, "Father, I have killed a few people."

"How many did you kill?" the priest asked.

He answered, "I killed only six persons, Father, but you will be the seventh if you can't escape."

37. IF WORSE COMES TO WORST

While delivering his lengthy sermon one long evening mass during Lent, the pastor, noticed a male parishioner sleeping. Wanting to give him a lesson or two, he stopped his sermon and loudly asked the congregation, "Those of you who want to go to heaven please stand up."

Everybody stood up except the sleeper. Then, after every one was again seated, at the top of his voice, the pastor shouted, "Anyone of you who wants to go to hell, please stand up!"

Startled, the sleeping man suddenly stood up while everyone else was seated, to the laughter of most of the congregation members. Then the pastor said, "You see, one of you was not listening."

The rebuked man reminded the priest, "Father, I didn't know what was going on because I was sleeping, but if worse comes to worst, you and I are both standing."

38. NOTHING CAN BE HEARD HERE

One day the pastor summoned his sacristan to the confessional box where he accused him of stealing money from the church. "Son," the priest said, "I've actually seen you a few times taking money from Sunday mass collections. So that God can forgive you, return the money you have stolen, and regret your sin."

The sacristan said, "Father, I can't hear you from my seat here. Why don't we change places?"

The pastor granted his request. Once the sacristan had taken his seat inside the confessional box, however, he immediately confronted the priest, "Pastor, more than once I've seen you kissing the woman who visited you in the rectory. God can only forgive you if you admit what you have done and repent of your sin."

The pastor responded, "You are right, my son, nothing can be heard from here."

39. YOU WILL LOSE WHOLE OF YOUR LIFE

A professor usually takes a small boat across the bay, to and from the university where he is teaching. One day during his boat ride, he asked the boat operator, "Do you know mathematics?"

"No, sir," he answered, "I have spent all my youth swimming."

"That's too bad," the professor said. "You've wasted a third of your life. Do you know anything about philosophy?"

"No, sir, for the same reason," he replied.

"That's terrible!" judged the professor. You've now thrown away two-thirds of your life!"

Suddenly, a huge wave capsized their boat. The boatman then asked the professor, "Sir, do you know how to swim?"

He replied, "Oh, no! All my life I have spent studying mathematics, philosophy, and other academic subjects."

"That's terrible, sir. Now you will lose your whole life!" declared the boatman.

40. THEY POCKETED THE DIFFERENCE

Little Lito wrote a letter to God asking for $50.00 to buy a toy to play with that he can call his own. He mailed the letter from the post office.

At the post office, out of curiosity two postmen opened the envelope addressed to God and read the boy's letter. Out of the goodness of their hearts, they chipped in $20.00 each and mailed $40.00 to the boy.

Days later, Lito received the envelope with joy, but when he opened it and found out that it was less than what he asked for, he was a little disappointed.

He wrote again a letter to God saying, "Dear God, thank you so much. I received the money you kindly sent me. But I beg you, Lord, allow me to point out that what I actually received was $10.00 short. Some postmen might have pocketed the difference."

41. SENIOR SAN VICENTE, TULUNGAN MO PO ANG PANGINOON (ST. VINCENT, PLEASE HELP THE LORD)

An old woman, a devotee of St. Vincent, was watching a live reenactment of the Crowning of Thorns during Lent. It so happened that the person playing the role of the Jew who crowned Jesus with thorns, had in real life been harboring hatred towards the one who played the role of Jesus.

He violently placed the crown of thorns on the head of the one acting as Jesus, who could not help but groan out of intense pain, prompting the old woman to shout, *"Senior San Vicente, "Tulungan mo po and panginoon!"* (St. Vincent, please help the Lord.)

42. GOODBYE, PANFILO!

After the pastor and his sacristan had left for a weekday service in a nearby town, the houseboy, without their knowledge, pretended that he was the new priest. Not long after he put on priest's habit, he saw a funeral march approaching the church. He asked the funeral march participants, "What is the dead person's name?"

"Panfilo is his name, Father," replied the dead person's relatives.

Then the fake priest said, "Before starting the services, I am passing around the love offering box. Be generous in giving for your deceased loved one." After pocketing the collection, he sprinkled the dead man with water from a pail as he was singing, "Goodbye, Panfilo, goodbye" to the tune of "Goodbye my teacher, goodbye . . ."

The fake priest was elated to get a positive compliment from those who attended the funeral service. Before leaving, one said, "Father, we like that you spoke our dialect in the services, unlike the previous priest who used Latin terms we couldn't understand."

43. WHAT A BODY

One Sunday mass during communion, Tony, a Catholic lay minister, always uttered the same phrase, "Body of Christ" to all communicants as he handed each one of them the sacred host.

But when a scantily clad sexy woman came, before handing her the sacred host, instead of saying the usual phrase, he exclaimed, "What a body!"

44. GOOD LORD, YOU HAVE DONE IT AGAIN

A priest was driving around the city when the police officer, noticing that the motorist was tipsy, asked him to pull over.

"What is in that bottle beside you?" the police officer asked.

"It's just water, Officer," the priest answered.

Getting hold of the bottle and smelling its contents, the police officer confronted him, "But this is really wine, not water!"

The priest exclaimed, "Good Lord, you have done it again, converting water into wine!"

45. OLD MOSES SAW THE YOUNG PRINCESS

In a journalism class, the professor told his students that in writing either a short story or novel, the elements of religion, royalty, sex, and mystery must be present to make the story interesting and exciting.

He then told his students that they had thirty minutes, to write a story at their desks, using no more than one hundred twenty words containing the said essential elements.

In less than three minutes, one young, creative student wrote, in thirteen words, the following:

"Old Moses saw the young princess was pregnant. What caused it, he wondered."

46. LOOK BUSY

It was reported that when the pope was informed that Jesus Christ had returned for his Second Coming and was on his way to the Vatican, he instructed his chief administrator, "Tell everybody to look busy!"

47. A GENTLER PARROT

A parishioner complained to the pastor that her parrot kept saying an embarrassing statement.

"What embarrassing statement does your parrot say?" the priest asked.

She always says, "May the bishop die the soonest."

"Don't worry," assured the pastor, "I will lend you my gentler and more religious parrot for a week, to educate yours."

When the two parrots were together, the parishioner, observing the interaction between the two birds, overheard them talking: The resident parrot, was as usual saying, "May the bishop die the soonest," answered by the visiting parrot saying, "Lord, hear our prayer!"

48. PRAISE THE LORD

A priest trained his powerful horse when to run and when to stop. When the rider says, "Praise the Lord," the horse runs. When the rider wants the horse to stop, he says, "Alleluia." He rehearsed his altar boy thoroughly on these appropriate horse commands before allowing him to ride his well-trained horse.

One day, the altar boy rode the horse. He said, "Praise the Lord," and the horse ran. A few minutes later, when the horse was galloping toward a cliff, the boy was scared to death. Luckily, he remembered to shout, "Alleluia!" prompting the horse to a sudden halt, right before the cliff.

But out of sense of relief and gratitude, he sighed, "Praise the Lord."

49. DISPOSITION OF TITHING COLLECTIONS

A Jewish rabbi, a Protestant minister, and a Catholic priest were comparing how they dispose of their tithing collections.

The rabbi said, "I just draw a circle on the ground. Then I toss all the collections up in the air. Whatever falls inside the circle belongs to God, whatever falls outside the circle belongs to me."

The minister declared, "What I do is I simply draw a line on the ground. Then I toss all the collections up in the air. Whatever falls on the ground to the right of the line belongs to God, whatever falls on the ground to the left of the line, belongs to me."

The priest declared, "In my case, I just toss all the collections up in the air and, what-ever goes up, up and away, belongs to God. Whatever falls down, belongs to me."

50. JUST CONFESS IT

Doy and Jim, together with their friends, attended a spiritual retreat at the church. During break time they left to have a snack at the cafeteria located across the street.

Jim told the group that he would foot the bill for all five of them. They all hurried up to eat.

It was raining hard, so they ran across the street back to the church. As soon as they got inside, Jim said, "I forgot to pay the cashier for our snacks, I must go back to settle my account."

Doy suggested, "Jim, it's raining hard. There is confession going on. Instead of paying, why not just confess it?"

51. THE ONLY ONES WHO CAN GO TO HEAVEN

Immediately after his death, Father Bruno, a Catholic priest, was shown around the different districts in heaven by St. Peter. The first district they visited was that of the Presbyterians, who were all consumed with joy playing violins. The second was that of the Jewish people, who were all in the state of ecstasy playing harps; the next was that of the Buddhists, who were blissfully playing guitars; and so on for all the other religious groups.

Father Bruno could not help but inquire, "St. Peter, where are the Catholics?"

"Ah, the Catholics," St. Peter answered. "They are all there in that area enclosed by very high walls. They still believe that they are the only ones who can go to heaven."

52. TOGETHER AGAIN

A priest, a lawyer, and a foolish man, Berto, had survived a terrible shipwreck and washed ashore together on an uninhabited island. As they were exploring, one of them stumbled on a bottle, out of which came dark smoke. It formed into a giant figure who loudly announced, "I am the good genie and out of the goodness of my heart I will grant one wish, and only one wish for each one of you."

The priest wished to be back in his parish and instantly he was saying mass in his church in Boston, Massachusetts.

The lawyer's wish was to go back to his office, and in no time, he found himself in New York City, practicing as a trial attorney.

After several years the genie, out of pity, approached Berto. "Your two companions have long been back in their respective cities. Are you not lonely here? What now is your wish?"

He just looked at the genie and muttered, "Yes, I feel lonely here. Bring them back!" Instantly, the three of them were reunited, to Berto's delight.

53. WHICH RELIGIOUS ORDER IS JESUS CHRIST'S FAVORITE?

An Augustinian priest, a Dominican priest, a Franciscan priest, and a Society of Jesus

(S. J.) priest were arguing about whose religious order was Jesus Christ's favorite.

Each one of them argued his case so persuasively that they could not decide on the winner. At dawn they saw handwriting on the wall, which said, "My children, it pains my heart that you are arguing whose religious order is closest to me. I assure you that I equally love you all." Below the message was signed: Jesus Christ, S.J.

54. WHO PRAYS THE ROSARY FASTEST?

A Filipino-Muslim and a Filipino-Chinese had a contest to see who could recite the rosary faster. For each mystery of the rosary, the latter recites one whole set of *Hail Mary* followed by *Holy Mary* then said, "the same" 10 times. The former recites one whole set of *Hail Mary* followed by *Holy Mary* then said "times 10." The Filipino-Muslim contestant handily won the contest.

55. THE PRIEST IN THE NUDIST CAMP

A renowned priest was invited to be the guest speaker at a graduation ceremony in a nudist camp. Before going to the camp, he reflected that we were all born naked, and that those nudists have no malice when they are naked, as, they are returning to our original state of nakedness and innocence.

So, he decided, in deference to those sincere nudist camp people, to get himself naked and without malice, just for once in his lifetime, at the nudist camp graduation ceremony.

Meanwhile, the nudist camp people had a meeting and agreed that they all would clothe themselves for the graduation celebration, out of respect for their distinguished guest.

Thus, on stage was a naked priest talking to his clothed 'nudist camp' graduation audience.

56. REJECTED FROM ENTERING HEAVEN

A man who had just died was rejected from entering heaven. He said to another person approaching the gate to heaven, "I was just rejected from entering heaven for not riding a horse. Here is my proposal to you: I'll pretend like a horse and you ride on my back. That way, both of us can enter heaven."

"Cool," the other man agreed, "let's do that."

But when they reached the gate of heaven, they heard the loud voice of St. Peter saying, "Let the man in, and keep the horse out!"

57. WHY JUDAS TURNED TRAITOR TO JESUS

One day Jesus asked his disciples to join him to walk for three days. On the first day, he asked them to carry a stone. While others carried heavier stone, Judas picked up a very light stone. At the end of the day, Jesus said to them, "You are all hungry now; the stone you carry will turn into bread for you to eat." Judas' bread was too tiny to satisfy his hunger.

The next day Jesus asked them to carry a stone again. This time Judas brought a very heavy stone. When they reached a stream, Jesus told them, "Throw your stone across the stream. Your throwing distance is a measure of your love for me." Judas could throw his large stone just a few yards into the water, while his companions, with smaller stones, were able to throw across the stream.

On the third day, our Lord asked them to carry two stones each. Judas played it safe this time, carrying one very small stone and one very large stone. He planned to put out the large stone for turning-into-bread purposes, and put out the small stone for throwing-across-the-stream purposes.

At the peak of the hill, Jesus said, "The stones that I asked you to carry will turn into your balls. Let us now run down the hill as fast as we can." Judas, with uneven ball sizes, had the hardest time going down the hill.

58. A LAST MEAL REQUEST

An Asian prisoner, who was about to be executed, was asked what was his choice of favorite meal to be served right before his execution. He quickly answered, "Noodles."

The warden asked him, "Why did you select noodles when you could have asked for much more delicious and nutritious meal—such as steak and lobster?"

His immediate reply was, "I just wanted noodles because they are good for a long life."

59. MAMON LUK (CHINESE FOOD WHICH SOUNDS LIKE 'MA, MOON LOOK)

'Mother, look at the moon' in Chinese is *mamon luk*.

60. *PADREROM, UNSAROM ISAGOLAROM TIYANROM BABOYAROM (CORRUPTED VISAYAN-LATIN COMBINATION, MEANING: "FATHER, WHAT TO MIX INSIDE A PIG'S STOMACH?)*

Before celebrating Easter Mass (said in Latin at that time), the parish priest instructed his houseboy to prepare a pig to be roasted by placing certain ingredients inside the stomach of the pig.

The houseboy forgot those ingredients, so, while priest was conducting the mass, after asking permission from the cantor, he stepped between them. After the priest had said some Latin phrases, the boy sang in response, *"Padrerom unsarom isagolarom tiyanrom baboyarom*?" (Father, what should be mixed inside the pig's stomach?)

The priest answered, *"Tontom, sagolarom sibuyarom, ahosarom, kamatesorom*." (Stupid, mix onions, garlic and tomatoes.)

61. PRAY AND SPRAY

The Philippines is a tropical country where it is hard to grow grapes. There were two groups of nuns belonging to the same religious order. One group lived in a rural area, and the other in an urban area. They both planted grapes in their respective locations. After a few months, the grapes planted in the rural area died, while those planted in the urban area survived and thrived.

The mother superior of the rural area group asked the urban nuns, "Why didn't our grapes survive, while yours are surviving and thriving?"

They replied, "We know that you pray for your grapes, just like we do, but we not only pray but also spray our grapes."

62. COMMITMENT AND INVOLVEMENT

After years of cruel and abusive masters, at long last Mr. Pig and Ms. Chicken were fortunate to have a kind and understanding human boss. On the eve of their master's birthday, the two planned to give him a surprise birthday gift.

"Ms. Chicken, what gift do you suggest that we give to our caring and loving master?"

After deep thought, she said, "Why not give him a hearty breakfast of ham and eggs? I will supply the eggs and you provide the ham"

"Great idea!" Mr. Pig observed. "We will give an amazing birthday treat to our wonderful master, worthy of his noble character: a delicious and satisfying ham and egg breakfast using the eggs coming from your own body, and ham supplied by mine.

But I got to tell you, Ms. Chicken, that this is a very tall order for me. While you can produce and produce eggs and remain alive, I have to die first to supply the ham. While yours is only an involvement, mine is a commitment!"

63. THE PRAYING LION

A missionary priest on his way to Africa heard about previous missionaries evangelizing even wild animals, which he could hardly believe. No sooner than he set foot in that continent, he found himself chased by an intimidating lion.

He stumbled, and was terrified as the lion pounced on him. The powerful animal then knelt and said a prayer of grace before his meal. "Bless us Oh Lord and this thy gift, which I am about to eat from thy bounty through Christ our Lord. Amen."

64. KISSING THE PRIEST

Right after the wedding ceremony, the priest said, "Now, the bride may kiss the groom."

The bride, who comes from the rural area in the Philippines, did not quite understand the priest's instruction, so the priest touched his own cheek with his fingers a few times. The bride immediately stood up and kissed the priest's cheek.

65. THE PRIEST'S ORDER

Three friends eating lunch in a restaurant saw a priest occupying another table. They agreed to have a contest to guess the priest's religious order. Whoever won would have a free lunch.

Their guesses, based on the color, design and belt of the priest's habit, were Franciscan, Dominican, and Augustinian.

To determine the winner, they asked the waiter to inquire on their behalf. As the three betting friends listened intently, he asked, "Father, what is your order?"

"*Siopao*," the priest answered. (Siopao is white bread with meat inside.)

66. NATURE TO LOVE

An old fisherman saved the life of a scorpion that was squeezed between two large stones. As he lifted the large stone to free it, the scorpion stung him before fleeing.

A young man who saw the incident took the old man to task saying, "Old man, you did not use your head! You should not have gone near that rascal scorpion that stung you mercilessly. Now, you are going to die because of your stupidity!"

Lying on the ground, the dying old man murmured, "Why should the scorpion's nature to sting change my nature to love?"

67. SERMON ON THE AMOUNT

A few church members, whenever their pastor reminds them of their tithing obligations, refer to his talk as the "Sermon On The Amount."

68. SUPER SPEEDING

A California Highway Patrol officer stopped a speeding driver. "Hey, I can tell you're a nun by your robes. Don't you know that you were driving at 101 miles per hour?" shouted the officer.

"Sorry, Officer. We're on Freeway 101—I thought 101 miles per hour was the speed limit, the driver replied.

"And your passengers, your fellow nuns, why are they all unconscious?" the officer inquired.

"Sir, they have fainted. We just came from Freeway 405!" the driving nun explained.

"For heaven's sake, why don't you proceed to Freeway 605?" the officer challenged her, teasingly.

69. IDENTIFYING MARKS

In his homily, a popular Filipino bishop, observed, "There are three identifying marks of a Filipino gathering. These are the three K's:

The first K means *Kainan* (Eating),
The second K stands for *Kodakan* (Picture Taking) and
The third K means *Karaoakehan* (Singing Along).

70. STAGES OF BROKEN MARRIAGE

The meaning of a Filipino word *ASAWA* is spouse. After several years of marriage, the first letter disappears, forming a new word *SAWA* meaning monotonous, or boring. This describes the mutual feelings at this stage of their marriage.

After several more years, another letter disappears to form another new word, *AWA* meaning pity, which is the only reason for their sticking together further.

A few years later, what remains is *WA* which means lost, or no longer around. This is when one partner has left their marital union.

Finally, all that is left is *A* (pronounced as "Ah") which is an expression of pain, of being deserted and abandoned.

71. FINISHED AND COMPLETE

A priest explained the difference between 'finished' and 'complete.' "When a man marries a thoughtful and helpful woman, he is complete. But when he marries a nagging and thoughtless woman, he is finished."

72. HOW WEALTHY WAS KING SOLOMON?

A Bible study participant, a married man, asked their teacher how wealthy King Solomon was.

The teacher replied, "If you doubt the wealth of King Solomon, get yourself another wife and see if you don't feel the financial pinch. Remember that King Solomon had three hundred wives and seven hundred concubines!"

73. TONIGHT IS THE NIGHT

At a conference for married couples, a lady social worker, advocated for frequent intimacy between a husband and wife. "The more frequent the intimacy, the happier the couple."

Three happy husbands gave witness on how many times they practiced the arts of love with their wives. The first said, "three times a week," the second, "once a day," and the third, "twice a day."

She observed, "You see, judging by their smiles, the first husband to give testimony is happy, the second is happier, and the third is the happiest. Thus, the more frequently a husband and wife get together alone, the happier the couple."

Then, the social worker noticed another husband at the back who had the widest smile. She asked him, "Why do you have that ear-to-ear grin? Are you intimate with your wife more than twice a day?"

He answered, "No Madam, we do it once a year."

"Then why are you so happy?" she asked, in disbelief.

Excitedly, he replied, "Because tonight is the night!"

74. BUSINESS ADVERTISEMENT

Doing business without advertising is like winking at a woman in the dark; you know what you are doing but nobody else does.

75. "GIVE THAT TO STUPID VIKTOR"

Viktor, John, and Virgilio, after exhaustive physical, psychological, emotional and mental tests, have tied in total scores among international candidates vying to be sent to Mars. To break the tie, the NASA director asked each one of them the same question: "If you were chosen to be sent to Mars, how much prize money will you ask for, and what will you do with it?"

Viktor said, "My asking prize is $1 million and because I am a patriotic man, all that money goes to my beloved country."

Next, John declared that of a $2 million prize, half of that money would go to his family, and the other half placed in trust for himself.

Finally, Virgilio, a Filipino astronaut, demanded a $3 million prize. The first $1 million will go to me and my family, and the second $1 million will be for you, Direk (for Director).

Though the NASA director was offended by the idea of bribery, for amusement sake he let the interview go on by asking, "Virgilio, what will you do with the balance?"

Virgilio answered, "Ah, the third million dollars? Give that to stupid Viktor. Let him fly!"

76. WHICH ONE IS MORE THRIFTY?

The Boholano and the Ilocano, both noted in the Philippines for their thriftiness, had a contest to see which of the two was more economical in using a manual fan.

The Boholano moved the fan from left to right in front of his face so slowly that it took an hour for the fan to travel from left to right and another hour from right to left; and back and forth.

On the other hand, the Ilocano held the fan steady in front of his face, which he moved quickly back and forth. The Ilocano was declared the winner.

77. SPELL "BOOKKEEPER"

A young boy from Bohol was asked by his teacher to spell the word, "bookkeeper".

He got in front of the class, bowed to them, and started saying in Boholano, "Bookkeeper: b, o, o pa *gajud*, k, *dugangan pa gajud* k, e, *dugangan pa gajud* e, p, *isumpay dajun* ang e r. Bookkeeper." (b, o, one more o, k, add another k, e, add another e, p, combine with e r).

78. PLATOON INSPECTION CONTEST

In preparation for the forthcoming platoon inspection contest, an ambitious platoon leader had his platoon members memorize the answers to the three questions he was certain would be asked. First, "How old are you?" Answer: "21 years old, sir." Second, "How long have you been in the army?" Answer: "Six months, sir." Third, "How do you like the food and service here?" Answer: "Both, sir." The platoon leader emphasized that the three answers be memorized in said order.

On the day of the contest, the inspector asked a soldier the three questions but in different order. In a loud, confident voice, he gave his answers in the memorized order:

1) "How long have you been in the army?" Answer: "21 years old, sir." 2) "How old are you?" Answer: 6 months, sir." The inspector, scratching his head in exasperation, said, "By golly one of us must be nuts!" Answer: "Both, sir."

79. WHO IS THE GREATEST MAN ON EARTH?

A tipsy G.I. (U.S. soldier) standing on the platform at Luneta Park, Manila, Philippines, in front of many people of different nationalities, waved a $100.00 bill and announced, "This money belongs to the person who can answer this question correctly: "Who is the greatest man on earth?"

A Japanese raised his hand and answered, "Emperor Hirohito."

The G.I. said, "Wrong."

The next to attempt was a French who mentioned, "General Charles de Gaulle."

"Incorrect," the soldier remarked.

A Filipino replied, "Dr. Jose Rizal."

"Not right," the U.S. soldier declared.

Finally, a Chinese stood up and answered, "The greatest man on earth is President George Washington."

"Genius!" the soldier remarked. "Come up here and receive your well-deserved $100.00 prize."

On the stage, the Chinese was congratulated. As he was pocketing the cash, he lectured the American soldier. "Actually, the greatest man on earth is Chairman Mao Tse Tung, but business is business!"

80. ANG IRONG BUANG (A MAD DOG)

Based on the audience's reaction, a competition judged which dog struck the most fear. The contestants were Doberman, Pit Bull, German Shepherd, and the lone entry from the Philippines, which was announced by an American announcer saying, "And the lone entry from the Philippines, Ladies and Gentlemen, is the 'Ang Irong Buang'!"

To the surprise of many, the *ang irong buang* was secured in a padlocked metal cage. It came out of the cage in chains, its tongue out and its mouth oozing with saliva.

The audience's body language and facial expressions showed they were afraid of the first three dogs.

But, when the *ang irong buang* was presented, Filipinos stampeded and ran away, a few of them climbing over the fence, making it the runaway winner.

(Fear of the ang irong buang is ingrained in the blood of many older Filipinos, particularly among the Bisayas or Visayans, due to its aggressiveness and its bite that carries rabies; and the past treatment of this disease required 30 days of painful anti-rabies injections).

81. AN OPPORTUNITY TO SAVE

After walking home from work, a man boasted to his friend, "Today, instead of riding the bus, I walked home. Had I taken that bus that passed me by, I would have spent $20.00. So, I am lucky to have saved $20.00 today."

His friend countered, "You are not so lucky! Had a taxi, instead of bus, passed you by, you could have saved $100.00!"

82. WHERE IS ALSO YOUR BATTLESHIP, SIR?

A first lieutenant/tactical inspector, and Jose, one of the cadets under inspection, used to be classmates in sixth grade. The former, who hailed from a well-to-do family, had the privilege to graduate from the Philippine Military Academy. The latter, dropped out of school due to poverty, and became a fisherman like his father. He was drafted under compulsory military training.

"Cadet Jose, what will you do if an enemy battleship attacked us?" asked the tactical inspector.

Jose, after careful deliberation, replied, "Shoot the battleship with cannons, sir."

"Wrong, there are no cannons," declared the tactical inspector.

"If there are no cannons, where is also your battleship, sir?" the cadet replied.

83. HIWALAY KUNG HIWALAY (GO SEPARATE WAYS IF THAT IS WHAT YOU WANT)

One day, the friends of a husband were so happy to hear him shout, *"Hiwalay kung hiwalay!"* (Go separate ways, if that is what you want!) They thought that their friend had at long last mustered the courage to stand up to his domineering wife.

They were disappointed when they peeped in and found that the husband was talking to himself as he was separating the white from the colored laundry that she ordered him to do.

84. BEATEN WITH *DOS POR DOS* (BEATEN WITH TWO-BY-TWOS)

Mr. Lim went to court to sue the person who had beaten him and rendered him unconscious. The judge interrogated him: "Mr. Lim, what did the accused use in beating your head?"

He answered, "He beat me with *dos por dos*, Your Honor."

The judge further asked, "What was the time when you were beaten?"

At this question, Mr. Lim became hysterical, and pointing at the judge he said, "You, Your Honor, you are stupid! You are really stupid, stupid, stupid!"

The judge was about to cite him with contempt of court, but Mr. Lim continued in broken Filipino, "*Ibig mong sabihin, pagkatapos tinamaan ang ulo ko ng pamalo, tingin muna ako lelo bago tulok*?" (Do you mean to say that after my head was struck, I looked at my watch before I fell unconscious?)

85. RECESSION AND DEPRESSION

The difference between recession and depression is that in a recession your neighbors are getting laid off, while in depression, you are the one getting laid off.

86. EGYPT, IRAQ AND IRAN (SOUND RESPECTIVELY LIKE 'A JEEP', 'A ROCK' AND 'A RUN')

A Filipino applicant applying for jobs in the Middle East took the screening tests given by the Overseas Employment Board (OEB) in Manila. Not knowing the correct answers, he answered three questions in a practical way based on the sound of the term asked in each question as follows:

1) Examiner's question: "What does Egypt mean to you?"

Applicant's answer: "Smaller than a truck."

2) Examiner's question: "What do you know about Iraq?

Applicant's answer: "Larger than a stone".

3) Examiner's question: "What is your understanding about Iran?

Applicant's answer: "Faster than a walk".

87. WHO IS MORE STUPID?

Two masters were comparing which of their houseboys is more stupid. The first master declared, "No houseboy is more stupid than mine. I gave him $50.00 to buy a Ford car so I can drive it. He accepted the money and, as he was leaving, he murmured, 'Is that all you want me to buy, sir?' "

The second master boasted, "If there is a stupidity contest, my houseboy would surely come out the champion. Imagine, I ordered him to go to my second house and check if I was there. He assured me before he left, 'I will go and check if you are there, sir.' "

It so happened that the two houseboys boarded the same bus. Now, seated together, they compared which of their masters was more stupid. "My master is the most stupid. He gave me $50.00 to buy a Ford car for his use," declared the first houseboy.

"What's wrong with that?" asked the second houseboy.

"He wants to buy a car when he has no driver's license yet!" reported the first houseboy.

The second houseboy maintained that there is no master more stupid than his, "He ordered me to go to his second house and check if he was there."

"And what's wrong with that?" the first houseboy inquired.

The second houseboy explained, "He asked me to go to his second house to check if he was there, when there was a phone in front of him. All he had to do was make a phone call, saying, 'Hello, hello, am I there?' He could have saved much time."

88. PATAY KANG BATA KA (CHILD, YOU ARE DEAD)

'Abortion' in Filipino is *patay kang bata ka*.

89. BANANA

Joe and Lester, best friends since childhood, found a $50.00 bill at the nearby park. Joe agreed to Lester's suggestion that instead of dividing their newly found treasure equally, just for fun, they would play a question and answer game. Lester would ask Joe three questions. They both agreed that the only correct answer to each of those questions will be 'banana'. If Joe can correctly answer each of the three questions, the whole $50.00 will go to him; otherwise, Lester will keep it.

Lester asked the first question, "What fruit is rich in potassium?"

"Banana," Joe answered.

"Correct," said Lester. He asked the second question, "What is a favorite fruit in the Philippines?"

Joe replied, "Banana,"

"Correct again," observed Lester.

For the third question, Lester held a banana behind his back with his left hand, and the $50.00 in his right hand. Then he asked, "Joe, which do you prefer to get, a banana or $50.00?"

When Joe answered, "Banana," Lester handed him the fruit. Had he answered $50.00, Lester would have faulted him for failing to give the agreed answer.

90. THE BOY WHO SWALLOWED TOO MANY ASPIRINS

A hysterical mother took her five-year-old boy to the doctor's clinic.

"Doctor, what shall I do? my son has swallowed twenty-six aspirin tablets!"

The doctor said in Filipino, *"Ibigay kaagad and sakit kasi nauna ang gamot* (Give immediately the sickness now because the medicine has come first.)

91. PAREHO NAMAN IYON – MGA WALANG LAMAN (THEY ARE THE SAME – BOTH ARE EMPTY)

Isang jeepney driver nahold-ap. (A jeepney driver was held up) *Sabi ng hold-aper sa kanya,* (The hold-upper told him) *Mamili ka, isurender ang wallet mo sa akin o e scatter ko iyong brain mo sa itong 45 caliber pistol ko?"* (You choose! Surrender your wallet to me or I'll scatter your brain with this 45-caliber pistol!)

Sagot ng jeepney driver, (The jeepney driver answered), *"Aywan ko, ikaw ang bahala. Pareho naman iyon – mga walang laman!"* (I don't know . . . it is up to you. They are the same— both are empty!)

92. "GIVE ME TORPEDO, SIR."

Shortly before World II ended, an American battleship landed at Camiguin Island, near Bohol, in the Philippines (now a lovely, beautiful tourist destination). Many of the island residents were so happy to receive 'relief' clothes from the naval officer.

An old woman going to the battleship asked another woman returning from the ship with a few clothes in her hand, "What do I say to ask for clothes from the American?"

She answered, just tell the American officer, "Give me torpedo, sir."

So, the poor woman told the naval officer, "Give me torpedo, sir." He was amused and surprised. The woman, holding and shaking her own clothing, insisted, "Give me torpedo, Sir!"

Sympathizing with the old woman and understanding her needs, he showered her with lots of 'relief' clothes.

93. THE LUCKY ONE

A patient, lying on surgery bed about to have a kidney operation, was congratulated by the surgeon. "Congratulations, lucky patient!"

"What do you mean, doc?" asked the patient.

The doctor said, "My mortality rate is 90% which means 9 out of 10 of my patients have died."

Terrified, the patient asked, "Then why are you congratulating me?"

The kidney specialist explained, "It is now late December. From January to November this year, I have operated on nine people and they all died on the operating table. Based on my track record, you could be the lucky one - the lone survivor from all my surgeries this year!"

94. THE SUREST CURE OF BALDNESS

If the cause of baldness is heredity, then its surest cure is to change your ancestors.

95. A BIRD SPECIALIST

An elderly couple took their favorite pets, a couple of birds, to a bird specialist to find out their gender so they could name them accordingly.

The bird specialist advised, "Feed the birds with worms. Be very careful to watch which worm is eaten by which bird, because the male bird eats the female worms, while the female bird eats the male worms."

"But, doctor," said the couple, "How do we know which worm is male and which is female?"

"I am only a bird specialist. Go and find a worm specialist!"

96. "GO AHEAD, I WILL FOLLOW YOU!"

When the office boss shouted at him, "Go to hell!" the wise subordinate answered loudly, "Go ahead, I will follow you!"

97. WHAT EXPANDS TEN TIMES WHEN STIMULATED?

In physiology class, the professor, pointing to a bespectacled woman, asked her, "Miss, what part of the human body expands ten times when stimulated?"

In righteous indignation, she said, "How dare you ask me that question!"

The professor then redirected the same question to a male student who answered, "The pupil of the eye."

"Will you elaborate on your answer?" requested the professor.

"In dim light, the pupil of the eye expands ten times," explained the student.

"Perfect," remarked the professor.

Returning to the lady whom he had called upon first, the professor said, "And now young lady, there are three counts against you: "First, you did not study your lesson. Second, you have impure thoughts. Third, the thing that you thought would expand ten times when stimulated does not really expand ten times!"

98. A PRESSING OBLIGATION

A young man has lots of clothes to iron. His friends have been inviting him over the phone to go out and join with them on their drinking spree. His consistent reply to each of them is: "I am sorry I can't join with you because I have pressing obligation."

99. DYING WITH SMILE

The FBI ordered an investigation into the mysterious circumstances surrounding three persons in the mortuary who have three things in common: a) They are all Filipinos, b) They are all smiling and c) They are all dead.

The findings were as follows:

1. The first person, had been smiling shortly before his death, having just won a multimillion-dollar lottery, but a traffic accident tragically ended his life.

2. The second person suffered a fatal heart attack with a smile while eating delicious *lechon* (roasted pig).

3. The third one, perhaps having the lowest IQ of them all, was climbing a guava tree when he was fatally hit by a lightning. He was smiling because he thought the flash was someone taking his picture.

100.   SPEAKING IN PUBLIC

A high school teacher gave a valuable tip to her English class students, saying, "Class, in public speaking, pattern your speech after the dress of a modern woman; it must be short

enough to be interesting but long enough to cover the subject matter."

101. DISPROVING A POPULAR SAYING

A wealthy businessman summoned all his sons to his deathbed. The eldest was a doctor, the second a lawyer, the third an engineer, the fourth an architect, and the youngest, an accountant.

"My sons, I am about to expire. I want to disprove the saying, 'You can't take material wealth with you to your grave.' Let's put up $1 million cash to put to my coffin. I will provide $500,000, and I earnestly ask that each one of you contribute $100,000 in cash."

Upon their father's death, each of the sons dutifully granted his request.

Before the burial, however, the youngest son secretly got the $1 million cash from the coffin and replaced it with his personal check, payable to Cash for $1 million.

ACKNOWLEDGMENTS

Grateful acknowledgment is made to the following who are instrumental to make this book possible from start to finish:

Consuelo Roa Jamora, my loving wife, for her inspiration and co-discernment with me in writing this book.

Ms. Carly Cumpstone, FriesenPress Publishing Specialist, for her patience and expertise in guiding me every step of the way in self-publishing towards complete publication of this book.

Mr. Brayden Sato, FriesenPress Art Illustrator, for the exciting, bold and fun book cover and inside art illustrations.

Nicole Barbosa for her assistance in initially conceptualizing the book cover design.

Our four precious children: Patricia, Nicolas, Joel and Clare; our caring sons-in-law: Eric Villanueva and Edmund Barbosa; and our half-dozen wonderful grandchildren: Esa Jamora, Nicole Barbosa, Jerrick Villanueva, Francis Barbosa, Patrick Villanueva, and Angel Barbosa – for encouraging me to write this book.

ABOUT THE AUTHOR

Along with his motto: 'Enjoy life — smile and laugh,' Juanito M. Jamora takes fun purposely. He has enjoyed bringing chuckles to people of every variety—in groups, at work, at church, and at many celebratory occasions in the Philippines and the US. He's one of those talented people who always has the perfect joke to offer. He knows that in any situation, if you can surprise people with a great punchline and get them laughing, they'll relax, welcome you, and open up to those around them.